POSTMODERN ENCOUNTERS

Foucault and Queer Theory

Tamsin Spargo

Published in the UK in 1999
by Icon Books Ltd., Grange Road,
Duxford, Cambridge CB2 4QF
email: icon@mistral.co.uk
www.iconbooks.co.uk

Published in the USA in 1999
by Totem Books
Inquiries to: PO Box 223,
Canal Street Station,
New York, NY 10013

Distributed in the UK, Europe,
Canada, South Africa and Asia
by the Penguin Group:
Penguin Books Ltd.,
27 Wrights Lane,
London W8 5TZ

In the United States,
distributed to the trade by
National Book Network Inc.,
4720 Boston Way, Lanham,
Maryland 20706

Published in Australia in 1999
by Allen & Unwin Pty. Ltd.,
PO Box 8500, 9 Atchison Street,
St. Leonards, NSW 2065

Library of Congress Catalog
Card Number: 99-071121

Series editor: Richard Appignanesi

ISBN 1 84046 092 X

Typesetting by Wayzgoose

Printed and bound in the UK by
Cox & Wyman Ltd., Reading

Sex Matters

There's been a lot of queer stuff going on in universities recently. Barbie, Shakespeare, even Jane Austen have been given a queer makeover. On the streets Bart Simpson is seen sporting a pink triangle, and the word 'queer', once hurled or whispered as an insult is now proudly claimed as a marker of transgression by people who once called themselves lesbian or gay. What's it all about?

A few years ago, the controller of Channel 4 was described as a 'pornographer in chief' because of the perceived sexual content of his programming. The world-wide web and satellite porn channels were seen as threatening to breach the defences of our island state of innocence. Now, it seems, everyone's at it, or rather talking about it. We've seen documentaries and dramas about prostitution, the vice squad, the sexual habits of every type of animal under the sun. If a programme has talking heads, chances are they'll be talking about doing it. And if you don't want to do it, you'd better keep quiet (celibacy's not sexy any more) or try Tantric sex. It's Madonna's latest thing, apparently, and she should know.

In politics, the old equation of power and sexiness still seems to triumph over principles and aesthetics alike. Although gay politicians are still being 'outed', being gay is not, it seems, the problem it once was for those with ruling ambitions. The press has repeatedly reported a growing climate of 'tolerance', as *The Sun* announced an end to gay-bashing editorials. Although gay and lesbian characters in soap operas are generally all too respectable, the flamboyant camp of Julian Clary and Eddie Izzard's transvestism have contributed to their success. It seems we're an altogether more open, more tolerant, sexier society – and it's getting better all the time. Or is it? Is mainstream culture just flirting with a bit of the other in order to keep us all on a broadly straight line?

While there does seem to be a broader definition of acceptable sexual behaviour, many of the old prejudices remain, and new crises are always in the making. Scenes of mob hysteria about convicted or even suspected paedophiles reveal the frightening side of people power. Freud may have uncovered infantile sexuality, but it's not something late 20th-century society can discuss rationally. There seems to be a crisis about how to cope with 'sex offenders' generally. Are they ill, and if so, what's the cure? Or are they 'evil'? What or whom are they offending? Nature, the Law, Society?

And how, more generally, do we know what makes one erotic activity good and another bad? Is it a matter of divine ordinance, biological nature, or social convention? Can we really be sure that our own desires and pleasures are normal, natural, nice – or that *we* are? Why does sex matter so much?

As the anthropologist Gayle Rubin argues: 'The realm of sexuality has its own internal politics, inequities, and modes of oppression. As with other aspects of human behaviour, the concrete institutional forms of sexuality at any given time and place are products of human activity. They are imbued with conflicts of interest and political manoeuvring, both deliberate and incidental. In that sense, sex is always political. But there are also historical periods in which sexuality is more sharply contested and more overtly politicized. In such periods, the domain of erotic life is, in effect, renegotiated.'[1]

If, as it seems, we are living in such a moment, then one of the ways in which erotic life is currently being renegotiated is through the exploration of *how* we understand sex in the ways we do. While this exploration may be going on in a myriad of contexts – in the media, in medicine, in parliament – the analysis which is the focus of this essay has been undertaken most energetically by individuals and groups who have experienced the fullest, and at times deadliest, effects of the politics of sex. As women were the first group to explore gender difference, so lesbians, gay men and other groups whose sexualities are defined against the norm of heterosexuality have been foremost in the exploration of the politics of sexuality. In challenging our most basic assumptions about sex, gender and sexuality, including the oppositions between heterosexual and homosexual, biological sex and culturally determined gender, and man and woman, these thinkers are developing new ways of exploring the issue of human identity.

Who is Foucault?

Michel Foucault (1926–84), philosopher, historian and activist, was one of the most influential of the thinkers whose work is generally categorised as poststructuralist. Together with Jacques Derrida's critiques of Western metaphysics and Jacques Lacan's radical re-articulation of psychoanalytic theory, Foucault's diverse inquiries into knowledge and power have formed the paradoxically destabilising foundation for much recent work on the status of the human subject.

Foucault was also a gay man who died of AIDS in 1984. After his death, his life and work were subject to a series of attacks which, claiming to seek the 'truth' of Foucault, salaciously and disapprovingly connected his supposed sadomasochistic preferences and practices with a (reductive) reading of the politics of his historical and philosophical writings. Foucault's work and life, achievements and demonisation, have made him a powerful model for many gay, lesbian and other intellectuals, and his analysis of the interrelationships of knowledge, power and sexuality was the most important intellectual catalyst of queer theory.

What is Queer Theory?

'Queer' can function as a noun, an adjective or a verb, but in each case is defined against the 'normal' or normalising. Queer theory is not a singular or systematic conceptual or methodological framework, but a collection of intellectual engagements with the relations between sex, gender and sexual desire. If queer theory is a school of thought, then it's one with a highly unorthodox view of discipline. The term describes a diverse range of critical practices and priorities: readings of the representation of same-sex desire in literary texts, films, music, images; analyses of the social and political power relations of sexuality; critiques of the sex-gender system; studies of transsexual and transgender identification, of sadomasochism and of transgressive desires.

A Queer Genealogy

This essay will consider some of the ways in which queer theory and thinking turns around and on Foucault, as writers working within a range of academic disciplines deploy and develop his ideas on sexuality and society.

Foucault can be seen as a catalyst, as a point of departure, an example and antecedent but also as a continuing irritant, a bit of grit that is still provoking the production of new ideas. As a narrative, the essay will inevitably present a type of linear history of Foucault's work and of the development of queer theory, but where possible I will try to avoid the seductions of the myths of simple causality and progress. Foucault is not the origin of queer theory, nor is queer theory the destination of Foucault's thinking. To use one of Foucault's own terms, the essay could be seen as a brief and partial 'genealogy'* of a particular set of discourses on sexuality culminating (temporarily and not exclusively) in the current queer moment.

Sex, Truth and Discourse

The first volume of Michel Foucault's *History of Sexuality* was written in the 1970s, towards the end of the so-called 'sexual revolution' in

*See the 'Key Ideas' section at the end of this book for an explanation of this and other terms.

Western culture. It offered a powerful and provocative counter-narrative to the long-established story about Victorian sexual repression giving way to progressive liberation and enlightenment in the 20th century. It was the beginning of Foucault's most ambitious project, one which was to be left unfinished at the time of his death.

In traditional accounts, sexuality is viewed as a natural feature of human life which was repressed in Western society and culture from the 17th century onwards, hidden from view like Victorian piano legs and unmentionable, censored out of speech and writing. Sexuality was still there, simmering under the prim surface of 19th-century bourgeois respectability, but it was stifled by prohibitions and repressions. Until, that is, it, and we, were liberated in the age of the mini-skirt and the analyst, revealing our legs and our innermost desires, bringing it all out into the open. Problems would remain, of course, and some of us would be happier and healthier than others in direct proportion to the free expression we were able to give to our happy and healthy sexual desires. But help was at hand for those with problems. The therapist, the analyst, the counsellor could help us to straighten ourselves out. A happy outcome to a sorry tale of the restriction of human potential. But is this story, familiar and comforting as it is, true? Has sexuality always been waiting for us to free it, and with it ourselves, from social constraints?

Foucault rejected this 'repressive hypothesis' and claimed that evidence from the 19th century pointed not to a prohibition on speaking about sexuality but to a remarkable proliferation of discourses about sexuality. So what was, is, sexuality? A vital feature of Foucault's argument is that sexuality is not a natural feature or fact of human life but a constructed category of experience which has historical, social and cultural, rather than biological, origins. This conception of sexuality is difficult to grasp; it seems counter-intuitive. Sexuality seems, like gender, to be simply *there*, but also to be somehow special, personal, a matter of our 'innermost desires' – who we want, what we want, how we want. It's something inside us, a property, *our* property. But having so much invested in believing sexuality to be natural doesn't mean that it is.

This does not mean that Foucault ruled out any biological dimension, but rather that he prioritised the crucial role of institutions and discourses in the formation of sexuality. As David Halperin, author of *Saint Foucault: Towards a Gay Hagiography*, notes, Foucault did not comment explicitly on the causes of same-sex desires. When asked about the distinction between innate predisposition to homosexuality and social conditioning, his response was: 'On this question I have absolutely nothing to say. "No comment."'[2] Instead of pursuing the illusory 'truth' of human sexuality, Foucault set out to examine its production. His concern was less with what 'sexuality' is, than with how it functions in society.

Scientia Sexualis

While psychoanalysts encouraged their patients to explore the sexual secrets that might hold the key to their mental and emotional health, Foucault set about exploring the ways in which psychoanalysis (among many other discourses), invites, or more properly incites, us to *produce* a knowledge about our sexuality which is itself cultural rather than natural and which contributes to the maintenance of specific power relations.

Psychoanalysis can be seen as the latest of a wide range of discursive practices that have sought not to silence or repress sexuality but to make people speak about it (and so themselves) in particular ways. The '*scientia sexualis*' of the West, as Foucault called it (in contrast to the '*ars erotica*' of cultures like China, Japan, India and the Roman Empire, which was based on multiplying pleasures), was fixated on finding the (shameful) truth about sexuality and used the process of *confession* as its key method of finding it. From the Christian confession, through medical, judicial, pedagogical and familial practices to the contemporary science of psychoanalysis, a history can be traced of men and women, boys and girls scrutinising their desires, emotions and thoughts, past and present, and telling someone about them. Telling the priest about their sins, describing their symptoms to the doctor, undergoing the talking cure: confessing sins, confessing diseases, confessing crimes, confessing the truth. And the truth was sexual.

In all of these confessional scenes, the speaker produces a narrative about his or her sexuality which is interpreted by a figure of authority. The 'truth' that is revealed in this process is, of course, not found but produced. It exists as knowledge within a particular discourse and is bound up with power. As in all of Foucault's work, power is understood as a matter of complex relationships rather than as a property inherent in a particular individual or class. So what, he asked, was at stake in the construction of sexuality at different historical moments? How did power circulate through the production of knowledge about sex?

From the 18th century onwards, Foucault argued, sexuality was regarded as something to be regulated and administered rather than judged. The Church and the Law had long been concerned with the regulation of sexuality, but in the Age of Enlightenment new governmental regimes were developed which focused on the embodied and sexual individual. Modified, secular versions of the confession were at the heart of a variety of techniques for internalising social norms. It was in this context that many of the ways of understanding sexuality that are still dominant today, including the opposition between homosexuality and heterosexuality, began to be formulated.

The Construction of Homosexuality

One of Foucault's most provocative assertions, and certainly one that acted as a catalyst for the development of queer theory, was that modern homosexuality is of comparatively recent origin. Many historians of homosexuality had been keen to trace connections and continuities between 20th-century homosexual identities and behaviours and those of earlier periods. Foucault, in contrast, insisted that the category of the homosexual grew out of a particular context in the 1870s and that, like sexuality generally, it must be viewed as a *constructed* category of knowledge rather than as a *discovered* identity.

Foucault did not suggest that sexual relationships between people of the same sex did not exist before the 19th century. In the Renaissance period, for example, sexual practices such as sodomy were condemned by the Church and prohibited by law, whether between men and men or men and women. But the crucial difference between this early form of regulating sexual practices and that of the late 19th century lies in the latter's claim to identify what Foucault called a 'species', an aberrant type of human being defined by perverse sexuality. So while 16th-century men and women might be urged to confess that they had indulged in shameful sexual practices against the law of God and the land, the late 19th-century man engaging in a sexual relationship with another man would be seen, and be encouraged to see himself, as 'homosexual'.

Along with a group of other types of subject whose sexuality was of particular interest or concern to 19th-century medical science (including women, children, the working classes), the 'homosexual' became a focus for a variety of studies and strategies. These 'technologies of sex' were designed to preserve and foster a productive and procreative population (or workforce) that met the needs of a developing capitalist system. The key unit of this social order was the bourgeois family within which the future workforce would be produced. This led, for example, to an unparalleled interest in the 'problem' of childhood masturbation, and a proliferation of texts and strategies for controlling children's sexual behaviour. Within this reproductive framework, same-sex desires and practices were a problem to be dealt with, aberrations from the procreative norm.

The homosexual was the subject of, and subject to, systematic inquiry in a wide range of discursive fields including demography, education and the law, which were concerned with protecting the health and purity of the population. While the man or woman confessing to sodomy in the 16th century would be convinced of the sinfulness of the act, the emphasis in the case of the 19th-century homosexual was not on actions but on the 'scientifically' determined *condition* of the individual. In Foucault's words: 'Homosexuality appeared as one of the forms of sexuality when it was transposed from the practice of sodomy onto a kind of interior androgyny, a hermaphrodism of the soul. The sodomite had been a temporary aberration; the homosexual was now a species.'[3] And the homosexual was seen as being totally suffused with sexuality: 'It was everywhere present in him: at the root of all his actions.'[4]

Power and Resistance

The negative aspects of the construction of homosexuality in the late 19th and early 20th centuries are obvious. The fact that a subject position or identity is constructed does not make it any less real for the identified. The homosexual was pathologised as a perverse or deviant type, a case of arrested development, a suitable case for treatment, in short as an aberration from a heterosexual norm. As such, he was subject to the disciplining, marginalising and subordinating effects of social control. Foucault has been criticised for having a conservative model of power, but actually he viewed it as always producing and never quite containing resistance: 'There are no relations of power without resistances; the latter are all the more real and effective because they are formed right at the point where relations of power are exercised; resistance to power does not have to come from elsewhere to be real, nor is it inexorably frustrated through being the compatriot of power . . .'[5]

A crucial feature of Foucault's analysis is his emphasis on the production of 'reverse discourse': 'There is no question that the appearance in nineteenth-century psychiatry, jurisprudence, and literature of a whole series of discourses on the species and subspecies of homosexuality, inversion, pederasty, and "psychic herm-aphrodism" made possible a strong advance of social controls into this area of "perversity"; but it also made possible the formation of a "reverse" discourse: homosexuality began to speak in its own behalf, to demand that its legitimacy or "naturality" be acknowledged, often in the same vocabulary, using the same categories by which it was medically disqualified.'[6]

It is possible to see in this model of reverse discourse the germ of identity politics. Those who are produced as deviant subjects, 'homosexuals', may find a common cause, a common dissenting voice that turns confession to profession. The discourse of sexology, for example, produced the identity category of the 'invert' as an aberration from the norm, but it might also enable that individual to question his or her social and political position. It provided a vocabulary and knowledge which could be strategically used by its subjects. As recent work has revealed, there were a number of explicit attempts to redeploy the knowledge and rhetoric of inversion and of homosexuality to appeal for decriminalisation in the late 19th century.

But Foucault's analysis of the 'perpetual spirals of power and pleasure' that were produced in the discourses of sexuality cannot be easily reduced to a binary opposition of discourse versus reverse discourse.[7] The 'sexual mosaic' of modern society is a dynamic network in which the optimisation of power is achieved with and through the multiplication of pleasures, not through their prohibition or restriction.[8] It is difficult to view power except in traditional terms as a negative force acting upon individuals or groups, but Foucault's subtler analysis of its status as a relation that simultaneously polices and produces, demands that we think beyond a conventional political logic of domination and resistance. Power relations cannot be simply overturned or inverted.

A number of critics have noted that Foucault ends the first volume of *The History of Sexuality* with an invocation of a different future 'economy of bodies and pleasures' not subject to the 'austere monarchy of sex'.[9] Some have read this as a utopian moment. But if it is an act of imagining, then there is no reason to suppose that the imagined future would be an improvement. In the second and third volumes, *The Use of Pleasure* and *The Care of the Self*, Foucault analysed approaches to sex within earlier social and ethical formations that contrasted with those of Western modernity. He focused on Greek and Roman techniques of the self and their intersection with early Christian processes of self-cultivation. These were disciplinary practices by means of which individuals attempted to transform themselves in order to attain particular states of happiness, purity, wisdom, perfection or immortality. In Greco-Roman culture, desire and sexual practices were viewed as ethical or moral concerns, but not as the ultimate shameful or repressed truth of human experience, as they would later be. Crucially, ethics was seen as a relation between the individual and itself, and not as the basis for standards or norms of behaviour; and discipline was seen as part of a practice aimed at attaining individual freedom or autonomy rather than subordinating others. While Greek and Roman societies differed from each other, the latter placing greater emphasis on hetero-sexuality and marriage, Christian culture effec-tively broke with the entire model of ethics of the classical world. Christianity, according to Foucault, developed universal moral codes and interdictions increasingly centred on the *truth of sex*. While Romans might have seen desire as potentially harmful, Christians viewed it as intrinsically evil.

At times, Foucault seemed to write approv-ingly of the non-normalising culture of ancient Greece in particular, but he was emphatic in his refusal to offer it as an alternative to contem-porary society. Restrictions on who could be an individual within the ethical domain – free men, not women or slaves – and unequal power relations such as those between penetra-tor and penetrated, revealed the persistence of forms of domination that could not be described as products of self-mastery.

Although some critics have recently turned to these later studies in order to explore the possibilities of non-normalising sexual and ethical practices, it was Foucault's overall model of the discursive construction of sexualities that was the main initial catalyst for queer theory.

Reactions to Foucault

Foucault was not the first to argue that sexuality is socially constructed, but from the 1980s onwards his work undeniably had the most impact and influence on new developments in gay and lesbian studies and on cultural studies of sexuality. Many aspects of his narrative have been revised, modified and challenged: historians have offered more attentive analyses of same-sex relationships and emergent related-identity categories in the early modern period; 19th-century taxonomies of inversion and homosexuality have been differentiated more precisely. His overall approach has also been subject to criticism, notably the Eurocentrism of his historical focus and his concentration on the history of male sexuality.

Foucault's ideas clearly paved the way for a different approach to understanding the relationships between sex, sexuality and power. But no intellectual work exists in total isolation from a broader cultural context, and the politics of sexual difference in the 1970s and 1980s was arguably as much part of the experience that led to the development of queer theory as was Foucault's analytical model. The history of activism during this period can also offer concrete examples of the operations of power identified by Foucault.

Foucault + ? = Queer Theory?

In the 1970s, when Foucault was writing his *History*, the term 'homosexual' was still employed in medical and legal discourses, but people were increasingly defining themselves as 'lesbian' or 'gay'. 'Gay', a term used for women of dubious repute in the 19th century, was appropriated as an alternative to 'homo-sexual' in the 1960s, much to the consternation of some people who bemoaned the corruption of an 'innocent' word. The most obvious difference between 'gay' and 'lesbian' and earlier categories was that instead of being assigned a passive position as an object of knowledge, lesbian- or gay-identified subjects were ostensibly choosing or claiming a position. Being gay or lesbian was a matter of pride, not of pathology; of resistance, not of self-effacement. As women's liberation challenged dominant constructions of femaleness as inferior, passive, secondary, so gay liberation contested the representation of same-sex desires and relationships as unnatural, deviant or incomplete.

In the mid-1970s, the movement's goal was to transform the social system seen as the cause of oppression. As some feminists criticised institutions like marriage and the family for supporting the oppression of women, and pressed for radical, even revolutionary social change, so too did the gay liberation movement. Both had strong, although by no means universal, affiliations with left-wing politics, and could be seen as running parallel with Marxist, socialist and feminist approaches in academia.

But the model of liberation through transforming the system gave way during the late 1970s to a different conception of gay and lesbian politics that had more in common with what is known as the 'ethnic' model. This presented gays and lesbians as a distinctive minority group, equal but different, and worked to achieve rights and legal protection within the existing order.

The achievements of this approach were considerable, and the basic model is still influential today. In addition to campaigns for justice and equal rights, groups such as the Campaign for Homosexual Equality in Britain and Gay Activists Alliance in the United States were actively involved in the promotion of 'positive' images of gayness. This included criticism of negative, homophobic images in the media, including the popular camp stereotypes of sitcoms which were seen as damaging (queering?) the image of gay and lesbian people. The promotion of images and narratives of self-worth, pleasure and style may have advanced the prospects of groups or individuals whose positive image fitted in with straight mainstream culture. Campaigns and alliances could also be seen as community-building, offering gays and lesbians a culture to call home.

To come home, of course, you first had to 'come out'. For lesbians and gay men, being 'out' or 'in the closet' became a crucial marker of their sexual politics. Coming out suggested emerging from confinement and concealment into the open, a movement from secrecy to public affirmation. So were visibly queer men and women in or out? What about people who didn't fit the image, who weren't at home in the positive, confident, upwardly mobile world of assimilationist politics and culture? And what about the acts, pleasures and identifications that were the cause of dissent and conflict within gay communities rather than the occasion of feel-good collective self-affirmation? Bisexuality, transsexuality, sadomasochism and transgender identification all implicitly challenged the inclusive ideal of assimilationist politics. The incompatibility can be partly interpreted in terms of respectability. If you want to be an equal part of a straight world by proving how ordinary, how 'just-like-you' (but perhaps a bit more sensitive or artistic) you are, it simply won't do to flaunt your more excessive, transgressive desires or relations.

Throughout the 1980s, versions of gay and lesbian experience promoted within political campaigns were criticised for privileging white, middle-class values. Tensions between genders and between the imperatives of gender and sexuality also caused heated debates and revealed the frailty of the community model of gay and lesbian politics. Throughout the history of gay liberation, some lesbians had criticised the masculinism of mainstream gay culture. One strand of lesbian feminism developed a model of lesbianism as woman identification that prioritised political motivation over sexual desire. In a further twist, however, other lesbians, including feminists, felt that this desexualised version of female same-sex desire excluded them and implicitly endorsed a sexually disempowering notion of women. Disagreements culminated in what are known as the 'sex wars', in which lesbian sadomasochists, women in butch-fem relationships and anti-censorship feminists loudly contested the idea of a united lesbian sisterhood. While the mainstream conception of gay male identity acknowledged diverse sexual practices, including non-monogamous and group sex, it too was seen by some as promoting a restricted, respectable ideal of the committed relationship. So, while gay and lesbian politics gained considerable ground in promoting greater acceptance and in moving towards equality, the ideal of a collective identity was being shattered by internal differences.

Identity Crisis

Viewed retrospectively with the aid of Foucauldian analysis, the fracturing of the myth of a unified and unifying gay and/or lesbian identity can be seen as a product not simply of differences of personal and political priorities but of basing politics on identity. Even though gay and lesbian identities might be seen as culturally constructed rather than innate, they inevitably constrained as well as enabled. The central defining characteristic was 'object choice', preference for sexual relationships with someone of the same gender as oneself. This may seem to be self-evidently the marker of gay and lesbian identity, but as Foucault's *History* had shown, such an object choice had not always constituted the basis for an identity and, as many dissenting voices suggested, it was not inevitably the crucial factor in everyone's perception of their sexuality. This model effectively made bisexuals seem to have a less secure or developed identity (rather as essentialist models of gender make transsexuals incomplete subjects), and excluded groups that defined their sexuality through activities and pleasures rather than gender preferences, such as sadomasochists.

With the onset of AIDS, this already fractured collective was confronted by a new set of pressures. The popular discourses that misrepresented AIDS as a gay disease contributed to renewed homophobia and necessitated a review of assimilationist strategies. Acceptance was all too quickly revealed to be tolerance, which was swiftly becoming intolerance. This led, in turn, to a renewed but decentralised radicalism in gay and lesbian politics. New coalitions were formed between men and women, not on the basis of essential identity but of a shared commitment to resisting the representations that were costing the lives of those with AIDS. Perhaps most interestingly, in the light of Foucault's *History*, the impact of safe-sex education led to a renewed emphasis on practices rather than identities in thinking about sex and sexuality. What you did rather than what you were was the crucial issue.

In the development of these new political strategies, many critics have seen evidence of the forms of resistance to oppressive and normalising social forces that Foucault identified as more tenable than grand revolutionary projects. Among the groups set up during this period was ACT UP, which organised public protests about AIDS policy and rhetoric, invading the New York stock exchange, blocking the Golden Gate Bridge and interrupting CBS newscasts. ACT UP's strategy focused on resisting the effects of power and knowledge as they were manifested in medical institutions, welfare provision, insurance companies and numerous other contexts. The group has been described by the queer theorist David Halperin as the most original, intelligent and creative political embodiment of Foucault's strategic reconceptualisation of sex, knowledge and power.[10]

For many people, the experience of the AIDS epidemic shattered their understandings of knowledge and identity, revealing both to be inextricably bound up with the operations of power. AIDS might be viewed as having a similar impact on conventional understandings of subjectivity and sexuality as the Holocaust and the atom bomb had on ideals of progressive enlightenment. After the event, nothing could be quite the same again. It was in the context of AIDS activism and rejection of assimilationist strategies that 'queer' was redeployed in its current fashion both in popular culture and in theory. Influenced by ACT UP and other AIDS activist strategies, another grouping founded in

New York in 1990 signalled in its name and in its rhetoric the reappropriation of a term that until then had been predominantly linked with homophobia and prejudice.

'We're here, we're queer, get used to it.'

Queer Nation and affiliated groups like the Pink Panthers organised street patrols to counter gay-bashing, commemorated the victims of homophobic violence with street graffiti campaigns, and held anti-homophobic education sessions in straight bars. They also organised media and arts campaigns subverting right-wing and homophobic propaganda and imagery. Central to the groups' rhetorical and representational strategies was the word 'queer', the slang term used mainly in homophobic discourse but also by some homosexuals who chose the term before or instead of 'gay' or 'lesbian'.

Although its radicalism has been questioned

when compared with groups like ACT UP, partly on the basis of the problematic concept of the 'nation', Queer Nation's celebration of a name publicly heard as an insult connected with what some see as a real difference in the attitude of some lesbians and gay men in the United States (and in Britain) to their identities and to their social, cultural and political positions. Some critics see this difference as a matter of age, some of class or attitude to mainstream society. Whatever the catalyst, some people who found 'gay' and 'lesbian' inadequate or restrictive identities found in 'queer' a position with which they could identify. In popular culture, queer meant sexier, more transgressive, a deliberate show of difference which didn't want to be assimilated or tolerated. This was a difference that meant to upset the status quo, to ask why we assume Bart Simpson is straight.

It is relatively easy to analyse in Foucauldian terms the shifts in predominant identities from 'homosexual' to 'gay' and 'lesbian', to 'queer', and to see how each offered possibilities and problems for individuals and for political action, produced through relationships with dominant discourses and knowledges. The categories succeed each other, although there have been significant overlaps which a linear history occludes. Traditional accounts of the history of homosexuality have tended to downplay the importance of aspects of the past that do not fit the model of progression from repression to liberation, including queer subcultures like lesbian butch-fem communities of the 1950s. These subcultures, which preceded gayness, have more in common with current queer culture. But if 'queer' is viewed primarily as the basis for a new identity politics, then it too will necessarily exclude and restrict; the unease with which many people view the prospect of identifying as queer reflects this.

Queer(ing) Theory

Although in popular usage 'queer' is effectively

used as an additional or alternative identity category, queer theory cannot be read simply as the academic underpinning of this cultural moment. Queer theorists' disenchantment with some aspects of gay and lesbian politics is not simply a rejection of the normativity of those particular categories, but rather derives from a different understanding of identity and power. If queer culture has reclaimed 'queer' as an adjective that contrasts with the relative respectability of 'gay' and 'lesbian', then queer theory could be seen as mobilising 'queer' as a verb that unsettles assumptions about sexed and sexual being and doing. In theory, queer is perpetually at odds with the normal, the norm, whether that is dominant heterosexuality or gay/lesbian identity. It is definitively eccentric, ab-normal.

Queer theory employs a number of ideas from poststructuralist theory, including Jacques Lacan's psychoanalytic models of decentred, unstable identity, Jacques Derrida's deconstruction of binary conceptual and linguistic structures, and, of course, Foucault's model of discourse, knowledge and power. Predictably, it does not have a single moment of origin, but is often retrospectively identified as beginning to be crystallised at a series of academic conferences in the United States in the late 1980s that addressed gay and lesbian topics in relation to poststructuralist theories. The studies collectively called queer theory are mostly within the humanities, in history, cultural and literary studies and philosophy, although the topics include scientific, legal and other discourses. The writers generally share a common concern with the politics of representation and a training in the analysis of written and visual culture, from literature and film to political discourse. Many worked, and some still work, within the gay and lesbian studies programmes that have increased rapidly in number as queer theory has grown in influence.

The relationship between queer theory and

gay and lesbian studies is complicated. Some writers and teachers move between the two fields or adopt either term for their work as seems strategically appropriate, much in the same way that gay, lesbian or queer identities may seem appropriate in different contexts. But there are some who feel that queer is somehow encouraging people to overlook or dismiss gay and lesbian theoretical or critical work, much as they saw the emphasis on Foucault as occluding similar work by less fashionable historians. Many academics are, like Foucault, involved in different forms of political activism, and it may be best to understand the relationship of queer theory and gay and lesbian studies in Foucauldian terms as part of a dynamic network of different but overlapping fields of knowledge and discursive practice.

Queer Foucault

Some queer studies are continuing Foucault's

project by exploring the diverse formations of different sexual identities, past and present. Notable examples are David Halperin's studies of sexuality in classical Greece and of Foucault's own work, Gayle Rubin's ongoing study of the gay male leather community in San Francisco, and Martha Vicinius' work on lesbian identities. Queer theory underpins work on homophobic discourses and constructions by Cindy Patton, Simon Watney and others. Many queer studies focus on the relationships between gay, lesbian and dissident sexualities and cultural production. Those working in this field include Joseph Bristow, Ed Cohen, Jonathan Dollimore, Lee Edelman, Alan Sinfield and Yvonne Yarboro-Bejarano. The number of queer texts and authors has increased dramatically through the 1990s, as have university courses on queer theory.

In their attention to the workings of specific cultural formations and power relations, the more localised studies could be seen as the most Foucauldian strand of queer theory. But without wishing to underplay their importance, I want to focus in the remainder of this essay on some of the studies that have brought Foucault's ideas into a series of encounters with other theoretical and philosophical models in order to explore the norms and processes of normalisation that sustain the current sexual system.

One of the first topics explored by queer theorists was the opposition between heterosexuality and homosexuality, which was seen as operating at the conceptual centre of traditional homophobic and anti-homophobic discourses alike.

Heterosexuality versus Homosexuality

If homosexuality is, as Foucault asserted, a cultural product, then what is heterosexuality? And why is it viewed as the natural, normal sexuality? Why is Western society governed by what queer theorists have called 'hetero-normativity'? Human reproduction may require the contribution of sperm and egg from male and female but, as Foucault argued, sexuality is a cultural product that cannot be regarded as a simple extension of a biological process. Just as homosexuality is a specific cultural category, so heterosexuality must have a history to be analysed. This analysis could be seen as a political necessity: what is the use, what are the dangers, of accepting that there is no such thing as a natural, unified homosexual identity if the presumption of a natural heterosexuality is unchallenged?

Queer studies of this opposition combine Foucault's history of sexuality with deconstructive textual analysis. In her introduction to a collection of essays called *Inside/Out: Lesbian Theories, Gay Theories* (1991), Diana Fuss applies Jacques Derrida's notion of the 'supplement' to the analysis of the opposition of heterosexual/homosexual. The supplement (here homosexual) is that which appears to be an *addition* to an apparently original term, but on which the supposed original (heterosexual) actually depends. So heterosexuality could be seen as a product of homosexuality, or rather of the same conceptual framework. So how does homosexuality come to be seen as the inferior part of what might be an opposition of equals? No opposition exists in splendid isolation – all work through relationships with others. The traditional, mutually dependent but antagonistic, male/female opposition, for example, has acquired its hierarchical structure through association with others: rational/emotional, strong/weak, active/passive and so on. Heterosexual/homosexual is similarly caught up in a network of supporting oppositions.

As an example, Fuss explored the interdependence of heterosexual/homosexual and the related opposition inside/outside within dominant and oppositional cultures. In addition to the obvious division between heterosexuals being inside and homosexuals outside mainstream society, this dialectical movement can be traced in the rhetoric of being 'out', and this suggests its limitations as a liberatory project. Declaring oneself to be *out* of the closet of concealed sexuality may be personally liberating, but it entails acknowledging the centrality of heterosexuality as well as reinforcing the marginality of those who are still *in* the closet. It is impossible, in short, to move entirely outside heterosexuality.

As Foucault's work and the experience of some affirmative homosexual politics has shown, demanding the recognition of a distinct homosexual identity inevitably reaffirms a binary and unequal opposition between homosexual and heterosexual. So rather than attempt to move outside or invert the opposition, queer theory could be seen as examining the ways in which the opposition has shaped moral and political hierarchies of knowledge and power. Some of the most detailed work in this area has been done by Eve Kosofsky Sedgwick, the literary critic whom *Rolling Stone* called 'the soft-spoken queen of gay studies'.

Sedgwick's work does not offer a way beyond the binary, but has begun to unpack the ways in which the enormous conceptual privilege of heterosexuality is embedded in a broad range of discourses. In doing so, she reveals the extent of the promotion of normative heterosexuality's dependence on a stigmatised homosexuality. In *Between Men: English Literature and Male Homosocial Desire* (1985), Sedgwick examined the ways in which male homosocial bonding is structured around hostility to homosexuality. In *Epistemology of the Closet* (1990) she asserted that the 'closet' or regime of the 'open secret' associated with homosexuality has profoundly structured ideas about value and knowledge in modern Western society.

The fraught relationship between knowledge,

power and sex is revealed in the academic reception of some queer writing. Sedgwick's work frequently takes the form of case studies of literary texts, a traditional scholarly exercise. Her essay on masturbation as a trope in Jane Austen's *Sense and Sensibility* was the cause of much consternation in some academic circles in the United States, and is often presented as a symbol of the corrupting influence of queer theory on an innocent discipline.[11] Anxiety about the propriety of teaching queer, gay or lesbian subjects is clearly bound up with fear that the subject-topic may corrupt the subject-student. The most obvious example of this fear in Britain was Section 28 of the Local Government Act 1988, which prohibited the 'promotion of homosexuality' by schools. Although such legislation relied on a homophobic idea of innocent (and implicitly heterosexual) children being led astray, it does raise the question of *how* we come to see ourselves as gay or straight. If homosexuality and heterosexuality are categories of knowledge rather than innate properties, how do we, as individuals, learn to know ourselves in this way?

These questions are central to some of the most ambitious work within queer theory, which develops ideas from Foucault and other poststructuralist theorists into a new and contentious theory of gender, sexuality, the body and subjectivity.

Getting Personal

A crucial feature of Foucault's analysis of sexuality and of related poststructuralist and queer readings is that the individual is not viewed as an autonomous Cartesian subject ('I think therefore I am') who has an innate or essential identity that exists independently of language. What we commonly or casually think of as the 'self' is, instead, regarded as a socially constructed fiction (albeit a serious one), as a product of language and of specific discourses linked to divisions of knowledge. I may believe that I am somehow essentially and uniquely myself and that I am engaged in an ongoing, and often frustrating, process of trying to express myself and my meanings to others through language. But this belief, this sense of individuality and autonomy, is itself a social construct rather than a recognition of a natural fact.

In the same way that gender appears to be a founding component of my identity, so my sexual preferences and desires seem, and feel, crucial to my sense of who I am. In the late 20th century, I am likely to think of my sexuality in terms of a range of possible identities – straight, gay, lesbian, bisexual – which are themselves bound up with my gender classification. I may consider myself to be a gay man or a straight woman, but I'd have trouble thinking of myself as a lesbian man (of which more later!). What allows me to think of myself as having an identity of any kind are the very discourses and their knowledges that produce and police sexuality as well as gender. The words I use, the thoughts I have, are bound up with my society's constructions of reality; just as I see the colours defined by the spectrum, so I perceive my sexual identity within the set of 'options' determined by a cultural network of discourses.

What Butler Saw

Gender Trouble: Feminism and the Subversion of Identity by Judith Butler, published in 1990, is arguably the most influential text in queer theory. Butler explicitly develops Foucault's work in relation to feminist theories of gender in order to expose and explore naturalised and normative models of gender and of heterosexuality.

Many feminist critics had noted that Foucault's study had been almost exclusively of the production of the *male* homosexual. While some explained this by reference to an assumed authorial androcentrism, for others this could be seen as the result of the historical contexts he examined (such as legal discourses), which had ignored female sexuality. In either case, feminists worried that the importance of gender was being underestimated in some appropriations of Foucault's work. Although his work had usefully enabled work on sexuality to be pursued in its own right rather than as a subsidiary of gender analysis, the intimate connections between the two categories in modern thought constituted an obvious site of further study and intervention.

Butler's study restores gender to a central position in the analysis of sexual desires and relations, but not in order to preserve it as the basis for political solidarity. Instead, she adopts Foucault's argument that 'sexuality' is discursively produced, and extends it to include gender. She presents gender as a *performative effect* experienced by the individual as a natural identity, arguing against the assumption that the gendered identity category 'woman' can be the basis for feminist politics on the grounds that attempts to deploy any identity as a foundation will inevitably, if inadvertently, sustain the normative binary structures of current sex, gender and libidinal relations.

Gender, Butler argues, is not the conceptual or cultural extension of chromosomal/biological sex (an established feminist reading), but an ongoing discursive practice currently structured around the concept of heterosexuality as the norm of human relationships. Compulsory heterosexuality is installed in gender through the productions of taboos against homosexuality, resulting in a false coherence of apparently stable genders attached to appropriate biological sexes. This is why identifying as a lesbian man seems preposterous. But the connections are not inevitable or natural.

If sexuality is a cultural construct or category of knowledge, and if, as feminists insist, gender is culturally produced, then why do we assume that sex, conceived as a binary opposition between male and female, is simply there? At the end of the introduction to his *History*, Butler notes, Foucault argues that 'sex' itself is a fictitious category that has been understood as the source and cause of desire. The body is not naturally 'sexed', but becomes so through the cultural processes that use the production of sexuality to extend and sustain specific power relations. But the idea that the body is natural, of a different order to cultural processes, is powerful, as Foucault's own work unexpectedly reveals.

Butler returns to Foucault and discovers that within his overall argument is a recurrent metaphor or figure of the body as a surface on which history writes or imprints cultural values. This seems, to Butler, to imply that the body has a materiality that precedes signification, which she finds problematic, and she looks for a way of reading the body as a *signifying practice*. In the work of Mary Douglas and Simon Watney on discourses that construct the margins and boundaries of the body as dangerous (including those about AIDS), Butler finds a possibility for developing Foucault's analysis beyond its own boundaries and limits, and for exploring the body as a mediating boundary that divides inner and outer to produce the experience of being a stable, coherent subject. Instead of being beyond analysis, the body, like sexuality, may have a genealogy.

While Foucault generally approached psychoanalysis as a discourse to be studied rather than used, Butler employs ideas from Freud, Kristeva, Lacan, Wittig and others to explore the ways in which identity effects are produced through the differentiation of subject and Other and the production of a fictional interior core.

For Butler, it is through the stylised repetition of particular bodily acts, gestures, and movements that the effect of gender is created as 'social temporality'.[12] We do not behave in certain ways because of our gender identity, we attain that identity through those behavioural patterns, which sustain gender norms. The process of repetition is 'at once a reenactment and reexperiencing of a set of meanings already socially established; and it is the mundane and ritualized form of their legitimation'.[13] This theory of 'performativity' is one of the most influential, if confusing, ideas to emerge from queer theory or feminism in recent times. Like Foucault's analysis of the interimplication of knowledge and power in the production of subject positions, gender performativity literally destroys the grounds of political movements whose goal is the liberation of repressed or oppressed natures, whether gendered or sexual, but opens up possibilities of resistance and subversion closed down by identity politics.

Performativity is often misread as performance in a commonsense way, as a matter of choice, rather than a necessity if one is to have any intelligible identity in terms of the current gender system. This may be partly because of the main example Butler chooses of subversive parodic gender performativity: drag. Traditionally seen by feminists as presenting a stereotyped femininity, in Butler's reading drag's hyperbolic parody exposes the imitative structure of gender itself, making us look again at what we think is natural.

The misreading of performativity as choosing gender, like selecting from a wardrobe, may stem from a utopian desire to evade the compulsions of the binary gender system and heterosexuality that Butler identifies, or from the pervasive consumerism of contemporary Western culture, which is structured around the myth of free choice. It may also, it has to be said, be connected with Butler's difficult and sometimes opaque writing style, and with a desire for answers, for tangible suggestions.

Queer Knowledges/Queer Performances

The line of inquiry from Foucault to Butler has branched off in many directions within feminist, gay and lesbian, and queer theories and studies. Within queer theory, the critique of naturalised binary gender classification has been extended in work on transsexuals and transgender. Some analyses focus on the construction of the body within medical discourse and practice, while others explore the possibilities of different sexual-techno-bodily configurations in the age of virtual reality. Some work in this area seems extraordinarily utopian. But in extending the analysis of the construction of sexualised and gendered bodies within new configurations of technology, knowledge and power, such work is offering a counterbalance to the tendency to focus on literary or fictional representations in much queer analysis.

Another strand of queer studies that intersects with Butler's work, as well as with queer culture and politics, is the rereading of the sub-versive or transgressive potential of camp. While the misreading of performativity as meaning that we can choose what gender to be is completely at odds with either a Foucauldian or a queer understanding of subjectivity, the idea that some modes of hyperbolic perfor-mance of gender can be subversive has been successfully connected with camp. Camp, according to Moe Meyer, is the discredited but knowing and subversive language (in a broad sense) of a denied queer subject.[14] Camp per-formance actually brings that subject into being, as well as functioning as a cultural critique. This seems to connect directly with Butler's model of gender performativity and the possibility of its subversion through twist-ing or queering.

Both of these aspects of queer theory – the investigation of knowledges about sexuality and of performativity and performance – bring us back to the question at the beginning of this essay about what makes Julian Clary and Eddie Izzard seem subversive, while earlier camp icons were often regarded as reinforcing limiting stereotypes. For some, it may be a matter of the assertiveness or 'outness' of the performer/performance, but from a queer position that explanation is inadequate. It relies on a narrative of progress – from 'in the closet' to 'out' – and on a belief that individual motivation or intention is the determinant of their meaning. And, as Foucault argued, these are powerful cultural myths rather than truths.

It might instead be seen as a matter of different contexts. In the 1970s, the camp images of closeted or flamboyant homosexuals confirmed negative 'knowledge' about 'queers' that circulated in the media, while gays and lesbians were trying to assert a different knowledge about themselves. Strategically, therefore, camp had a different impact than it has today, when it can act as a queer subversion of respectable norms of either heterosexual or gay and lesbian identities and ways of being. But it's not a simple matter of camp now being of itself an inevitably subversive mode. Queer critiques of normativity cannot overlook the ability of dominant discourses and knowledges to appropriate and contain subversion.

The strength of dominant understandings of sex, sexuality and gender can be seen in the different reception of Clary and Izzard. Clary seems to fit predictably into a particular camp niche which he has successfully adapted to mainstream gameshow and sitcom formats. Reactions to Eddie Izzard have been rather more complex. While the comedian's transvestism still provokes a range of reactions from interviewers and commentators, it is his sexuality that seems to be perceived as holding the key to his problematic status within current models of gender. Izzard's own accounts of his choices and preferences have varied, but they are not really the issue here. His combining of conventional signs of opposing gender, like skirt and stubble, means he does not fit neatly into the manly=man=male or feminine=woman=female alternatives. In many conversations about him, this leads to the question: 'Is he straight, gay, or what?' His performance disturbs conventional knowledge about what gender conceived as either/or male or female looks like. So baffled observers turn to the other conventional couple, homosexual/heterosexual, in order to make sense of their confusion.

In this example, it is possible to see the dynamics of the discursive construction of gender and of sexuality as separate but connected. Izzard's appearance can be interpreted as the performative queering of norms of gender and sexuality, while reactions to it reveal the force of normalisation that pulls us towards conventional understandings of bodies and identities. In Foucauldian terms, we might read this as an embodiment of resistance 'inflaming certain points of the body, certain moments in life, certain types of behavior' and of our attempts to restore that body to its proper, knowable condition.

This type of resistance is not limited to the more dramatic aspects of performance. Queer theory and culture may stress the connections between theatricality and politics rather than seeing them as mutually exclusive, but there is a more 'sober' side to queer. In theory and in practice, queer could be understood as an adjective that acts as a performative, that has the force of a verb. David Halperin sees queer as a 'horizon of possibility' and the queer subject as occupying an 'eccentric positionality' in relation to the normal, the legitimate, the dominant.[15] Eve Kosofsky Sedgwick suggests that calling oneself queer involves 'undertaking particular, performative acts of experimental self-perception and filiation'.[16] There are perhaps echoes in these attempts to think about identities without essences, subjects in process, of Foucault's interest in the non-normalising techniques of the self in Greek culture. Halperin sees in Foucault's positive comments on the practice of S/M as a strategic game that creates pleasure rather than a form of domination, a pointer to a queer sexual practice that could open up the possibility of a 'more impersonal self'.[17] In general, some of the most recent work in queer theory is seeking to understand the relationships between identity and action in ways that allow for individual and collective agency in resisting oppressive knowledges and practices without returning to the modernist idea of the autonomous subject. Like some of Foucault's pronouncements, rather than analyses, this work has a utopian edge, but one tempered by recognition that the shape of the future can never be dictated.

Queer Today and Gone Tomorrow?

Queer culture and queer theory have recently attracted a great deal of criticism from lesbian, gay and queer activists and from academics. For some, the queer moment has already passed, its transgressive gestures transformed into fashion accessories. You can wear a nipple ring, a 'Queer as Fuck' T-shirt, watch queer films, but does it really make a difference? Has queer just become another identity category, pierced rather than fragmented? In the consumer society of late capitalism, are queers really just lesbians, gays and a few others whose most intimate relationship is with their credit cards?

Queer theory itself has been criticised for its abstraction, its fetishising of discourse and apparent contempt for the mundane. These criticisms echo those voiced against post-structuralist and postmodernist theories in general. More specifically, it has been accused of ignoring or underestimating the realities of oppression and the gains to be made by organised campaigns for rights and justice. Its interventionist credentials – political, intellectual and social – are seen by some as being undermined by its tendency to focus on difference and transgression as goals in themselves. A tendency in some queer writing to present gender and identity as almost exclusively negative, imprisoning structures or concepts has also invited criticism, and some commentators suggest that queer owes more to a masculinist gay identity than it acknowledges.

Inevitably, some criticism is based on reductive understanding. In the deluge of essays and books that claim queer status, some of the arguments of queer theory have been diluted or misrepresented to the point of absurdity. In some studies, queer theory's attempts to move beyond a constructivism-versus-essentialism impasse have been displaced by a refusal to view any genetic study as other than genocidally motivated. Judith Butler's model of gender performativity is regularly turned into an invitation to choose your gender with your daily wardrobe (an attractive utopian prospect, but one which does a disservice to the conceptual rigour of the original argument).

As an academic discourse, sustained within a university system that supports research while simultaneously defining its limits, queer theory is caught up in a double movement of contesting and producing knowledge, of challenging norms yet facing a possible future as a paradoxical orthodoxy. If queer becomes normal, respectable, if it becomes just another option, then it ceases to be queer. Teresa de Lauretis, one of the first to use the term, has stated that queer theory 'has quickly become a conceptually vacuous creature of the publishing industry'.[18] But while the term may now be deployed within distinctly unqueer projects, it is also being constantly reworked in changing social and discursive contexts. New intellectual encounters are diversifying the range of queer theory's subjects and methods. Although sexuality remains a key object of queer analysis, it is increasingly being examined in relation to other categories of knowledge involved in the maintenance of unequal power relations: race, religion, nationality, age and class.

While queer theorists renegotiate their terms of engagement with their subject, perhaps the final words should be Foucault's: 'The critical ontology of ourselves has to be considered not, certainly, as a theory, a doctrine, nor even as a permanent body of knowledge that is accumulating; it has to be conceived as an attitude, an ethos, a philosophical life in which the critique of what we are is at one and the same time the historical analysis of the limits that are imposed on us and an experiment with the possibility of going beyond them.'[19]

Notes

1. Gayle S. Rubin, 'Thinking Sex: Notes for a Radical Theory of the Politics of Sexuality', in Henry Abelove, Michèle Aina Barale, David M. Halperin (eds.), *The Lesbian and Gay Studies Reader*, New York and London: Routledge, 1993, p. 4.

2. David M. Halperin, *Saint Foucault: Towards a Gay Hagiography*, New York and Oxford: Oxford University Press, 1995, p. 4.

3. Michel Foucault, *The History of Sexuality: An Introduction*, Harmondsworth: Penguin, 1984, p. 43.

4. Ibid., p. 43.

5. Michel Foucault, 'Power and Strategies', in Colin Gordon (ed.), *Power/Knowledge: Selected Interviews and Other Writings, 1972–1977*, New York: Pantheon, 1980, p. 142.

6. Michel Foucault, *The History of Sexuality: An Introduction*, p. 101.

7. Ibid., p. 45.

8. Ibid., p. 64.

9. Ibid., p. 159.

10. David M. Halperin, *Saint Foucault: Towards a Gay Hagiography*, p. 122.

11. Eve Kosofsky Sedgwick, 'Jane Austen and the Masturbating Girl', in *Tendencies*, London: Routledge, 1994, pp. 109–29.

12. Judith Butler, *Gender Trouble: Feminism and the Subversion of Identity*, New York and London: Routledge, 1990, p. 141.

13. Ibid., p. 140.

14. Moe Meyer, 'Introduction: Reclaiming the discourse of camp', in *The Politics and Poetics of Camp*, London and New York: Routledge, 1994, p. 12.

15. David M. Halperin, *Saint Foucault: Towards a Gay Hagiography*, p. 62.

16. Eve Kosofsky Sedgwick, 'Queer and Now', in *Tendencies*, p. 9.

17. David M. Halperin, *Saint Foucault: Towards a Gay Hagiography*, pp. 85–93.

18. Teresa de Lauretis, 'Habit Changes', in *Differences: A Journal of Feminist Cultural Studies*, Vol. 6, Nos. 2 and 3, p. 297.

19. Michel Foucault, 'What is Enlightenment?', in Paul Rabinow (ed.), *The Foucault Reader*, Harmondsworth: Penguin, 1986, p. 50.

Further Reading

Judith Butler, *Gender Trouble: Feminism and the Subversion of Identity*, Routledge, London, 1990.

Michel Foucault, *The History of Sexuality: An Introduction*, Penguin, Harmondsworth, 1984.

Annamarie Jagose, *Queer Theory*, Melbourne University Press, Melbourne, 1996.

Eve Kosofsky Sedgwick, *Epistemology of the Closet*, University of California Press, Berkeley, 1990.

Michael Warner (ed.), *Fear of a Queer Planet: Queer Politics and Social Theory*, University of Minnesota Press, London, 1993.

Key Ideas

Discourse

In Foucauldian theory, 'discourse' is not just another word for speaking, but a historically situated material practice that produces power relations. Discourses exist within and support institutions and social groups, and are bound up with specific knowledges. So the discourse of medicine produces particular practices, knowledges and power relations.

Genealogy

This is Foucault's key term, derived from Nietzsche, for an inquiry into the development of discourses, which concentrates not on continuity or linear progression but on the localised, relational and discontinuous. It has been interpreted, by Judith Butler, as tracing the installation and operation of false universals.

Heteronormativity

This term specifies the tendency in the contemporary Western sex-gender system to view heterosexual relations as the *norm*, and all other forms of sexual behaviour as *deviations* from this norm.

Identity Politics

Affirmative political strategy based on the assertion of a

common cause through shared characteristics (viewed as either innate or socially acquired). Traditional examples of identity politics, based on gender or racial difference, have been the subject of criticism for overlooking the complexity of identity *formation*.

Lacanian Model of Subjectivity

Poststructuralist psychoanalyst Jacques Lacan insisted that our identities are formed through language, are fundamentally unstable and in process.

Normativity

A type of operation of power that establishes and promotes a set of norms (of behaviour, of being). While the 'normal' might be statistical, norms tend to be *morally* established and have the force of *imperatives*. Heterosexuality might be 'normal' in terms of statistics, but the normativity of current understandings of sex grants it the status of a norm, defined against *ab-normal* practices and desires. The most disturbing feature of normativity is the 'normal-isation' through which norms are maintained. Foucault attempted to define non-normalising cultures and practices, as well as exploring the normative and normalising.

Performativity

A term derived from the British philosopher J. L. Austin's speech act theory, in which certain utterances of ceremony perform an action and exercise a binding power. Examples include legal sentencing and the marriage ceremony. The concept was adapted by Judith Butler to describe the way in which gender is produced as an *effect* of a regulatory regime that requires the ritualised repetition of particular forms of behaviour.

Scientia Sexualis

Foucault's name for modern Western culture's inscription of the body within discourses of sexuality that produce knowledges which are both disciplinary and productive. These discourses have a normalising force, and are legitimised by a scientific 'will to truth'.

Taxonomy

A system of classification that imposes order on the world in accordance with culturally specific values.

Transsexual/Transgender

While *transsexual* usually refers to individuals who have undergone medical treatment, including surgical and hormonal procedures, to make the body correspond to the person's perception of themselves as male or female, *transgender* usually refers to those who refuse or disrupt the cultural norms of masculine or feminine appearance or behaviour and their assumed correspondence to pre-existing biological maleness or femaleness.

Other titles available in the Postmodern Encounters series from Icon/Totem

Nietzsche and Postmodernism

Dave Robinson

ISBN 1 84046 093 8
UK £2.99   USA $7.95

Friedrich Nietzsche (1844–1900) has exerted a huge influence on 20th century philosophy and literature – an influence that looks set to continue into the 21st century. Nietzsche questioned what it means for us to live in our modern world. He was an 'anti-philosopher' who expressed grave reservations about the reliability and extent of human knowledge. His radical scepticism disturbs our deepest-held beliefs and values. For these reasons, Nietzsche casts a 'long shadow' on the complex cultural and philosophical phenomenon we now call 'postmodernism'.

Nietzsche and Postmodernism explains the key ideas of this 'Anti-Christ' philosopher. It then provides a clear account of the central themes of postmodernist thought exemplified by such thinkers as Derrida, Foucault, Lyotard and Rorty, and concludes by asking if Nietzsche can justifiably be called the first great postmodernist.

Dave Robinson has taught philosophy for many years. He is the author of Icon/Totem's introductory guides to Philosophy, Ethics and Descartes. He thinks that Nietzsche is a postmodernist, but he's not sure.

Derrida and the End of History
Stuart Sim
ISBN 1 84046 094 6
UK £2.99   USA $7.95

What does it mean to proclaim 'the end of history',
as several thinkers have done in recent years? Francis
Fukuyama, the American political theorist, created a
considerable stir in *The End of History and the Last Man*
(1992) by claiming that the fall of communism and the
triumph of free market liberalism brought an 'end of
history' as we know it. Prominent among his critics has
been the French philosopher Jacques Derrida, whose
Specters of Marx (1993) deconstructed the concept of
'the end of history' as an ideological confidence trick, in
an effort to salvage the unfinished and ongoing project
of democracy.

Derrida and the End of History places Derrida's claim
within the context of a wider tradition of 'endist' thought.
Derrida's critique of endism is highlighted as one of his
most valuable contributions to the postmodern cultural
debate – as well as being the most accessible entry to
deconstruction, the controversial philosophical
movement founded by him.

Stuart Sim is Professor of English Studies at the
University of Sunderland. The author of several works
on critical and cultural theory, he edited *The Icon Critical
Dictionary of Postmodern Thought* (1998).

Baudrillard and the Millennium
Christopher Horrocks
ISBN 1 84046 091 1
UK £2.99   USA $7.95

'In a sense, we do not believe in the Year 2000', says French thinker Jean Baudrillard. Still more disturbing is his claim that the millennium might not take place. Baudrillard's analysis of 'Y2K' reveals a repentant culture intent on storing, mourning and laundering its past, and a world from which even the possibility of the 'end of history' has vanished. Yet behind this bleak vision of integrated reality, Baudrillard identifies enigmatic possibilities and perhaps a final ironic twist.

Baudrillard and the Millennium confronts the strategies of this major cultural analyst's encounter with the greatest non-event of the postmodern age, and accounts for the critical censure of Baudrillard's enterprise. Key topics, such as natural catastrophes, the body, 'victim culture', identity and Internet viruses, are discussed in reference to the development of Jean Baudrillard's millenarian thought from the 1980s to the threshold of the Year 2000 – from simulation to disappearance.

Christopher Horrocks is Senior Lecturer in Art History at Kingston University in Surrey. His publications include *Introducing Baudrillard* and *Introducing Foucault,* both published by Icon/Totem. He lives in Tulse Hill, in the south of London.

Einstein and the Total Eclipse
Peter Coles
ISBN 1 84046 089 X
UK £2.99   USA $7.95

In ancient times, the duration of a total solar eclipse was a time of fear and wonder. The scientific revolution that began with Copernicus relegated these eclipses to the category of 'understood' phenomena. Astronomers still relish their occurrence, not because of the event itself, but because of the opportunity it provides to carry out observations that would otherwise be impossible by day.

This book is about a famous example of this opportunism: the two expeditions to observe the bending of starlight by the Sun – predicted by Einstein's general theory of relativity – from Sobral in northern Brazil and the island of Principe in the Gulf of Guinea during the eclipse of 29 May 1919.

As well as providing a simple way of understanding the key ideas of Einstein's theory, this story offers fascinating insights into the sociological conflicts between 'Big Science' and popular culture that are as real today as they were 80 years ago.

Peter Coles is a cosmologist by trade, and Professor of Astrophysics at the University of Nottingham. His most recent book is *The Icon Critical Dictionary of the New Cosmology* (1998).